Geometry Workbook

3rd Grade

SPEEDY
PUBLISHING

Speedy Publishing LLC
40 E. Main St. #1156
Newark, DE 19711
www.speedypublishing.com

Lines, Curves and Shapes

List down objects you see that have **straight lines** on them.

Straight Lines

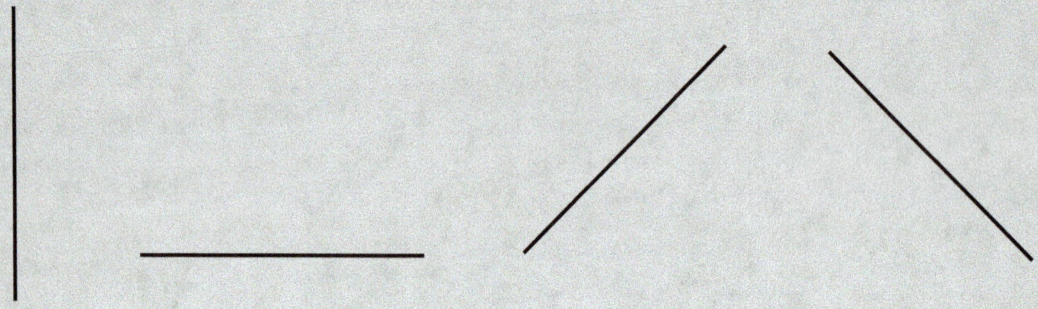

List down objects you see that have **curved lines** on them.

Curved Lines

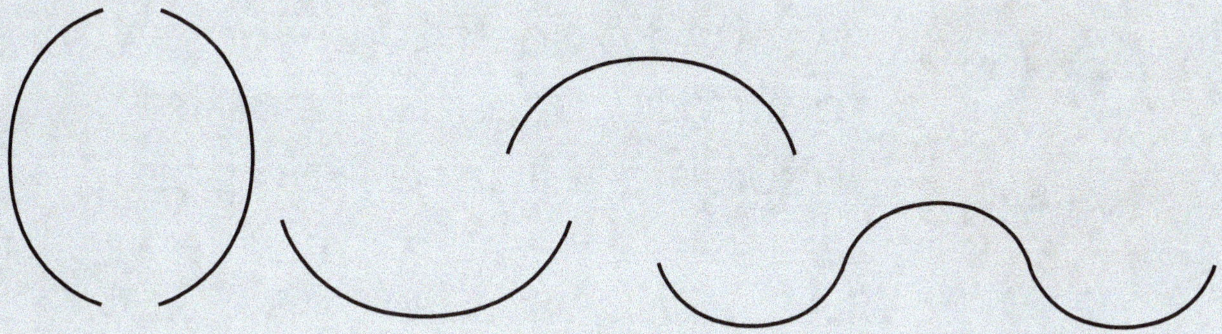

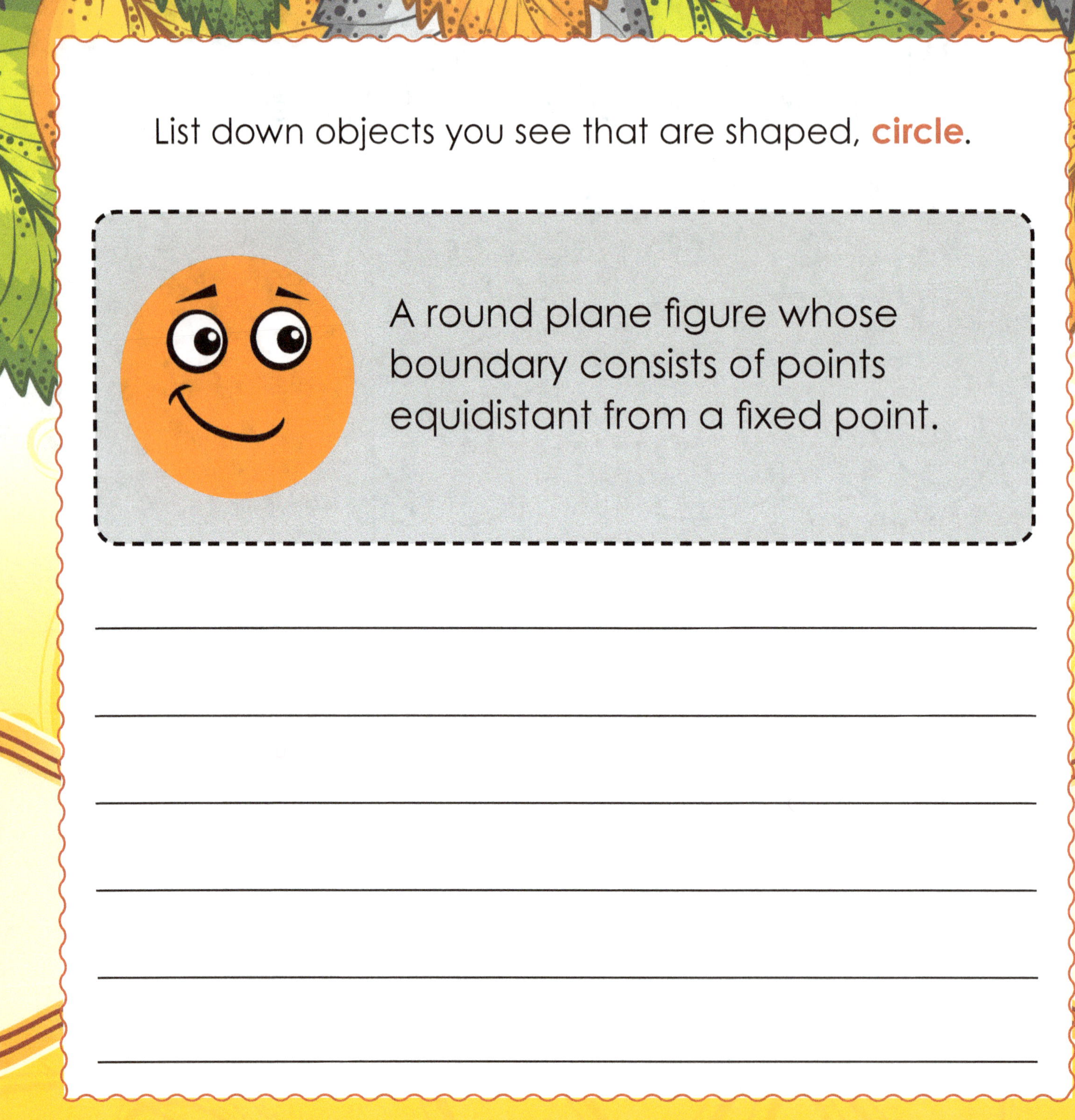

List down objects you see that are shaped, **circle**.

A round plane figure whose boundary consists of points equidistant from a fixed point.

List down objects you see that are shaped, **square**.

It has 4 straight sides and 4 corners. All fours sides have the same length.

____

____

____

____

____

____

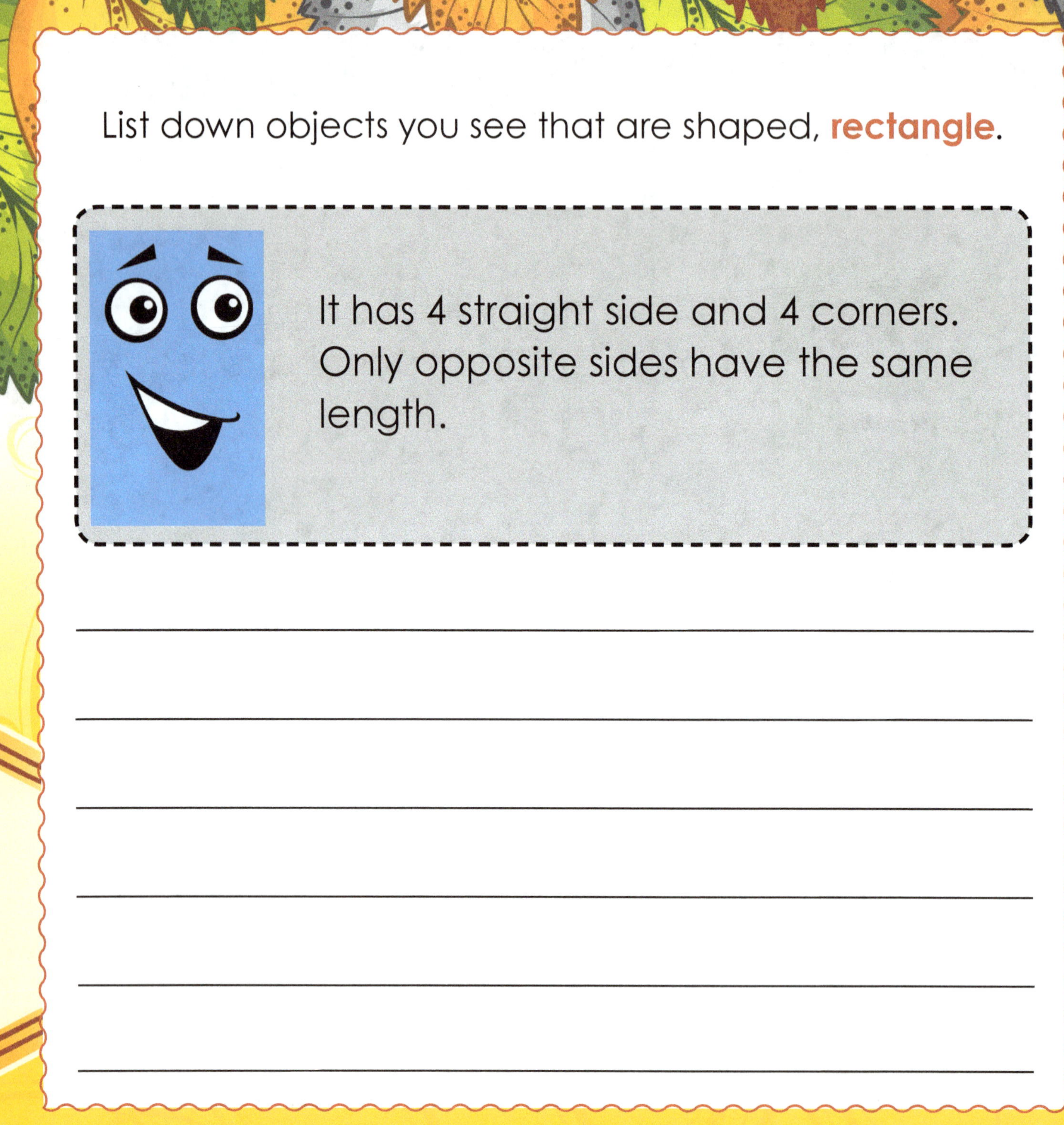

List down objects you see that are shaped, **rectangle**.

It has 4 straight side and 4 corners. Only opposite sides have the same length.

List down objects you see that are shaped, **pentagon**.

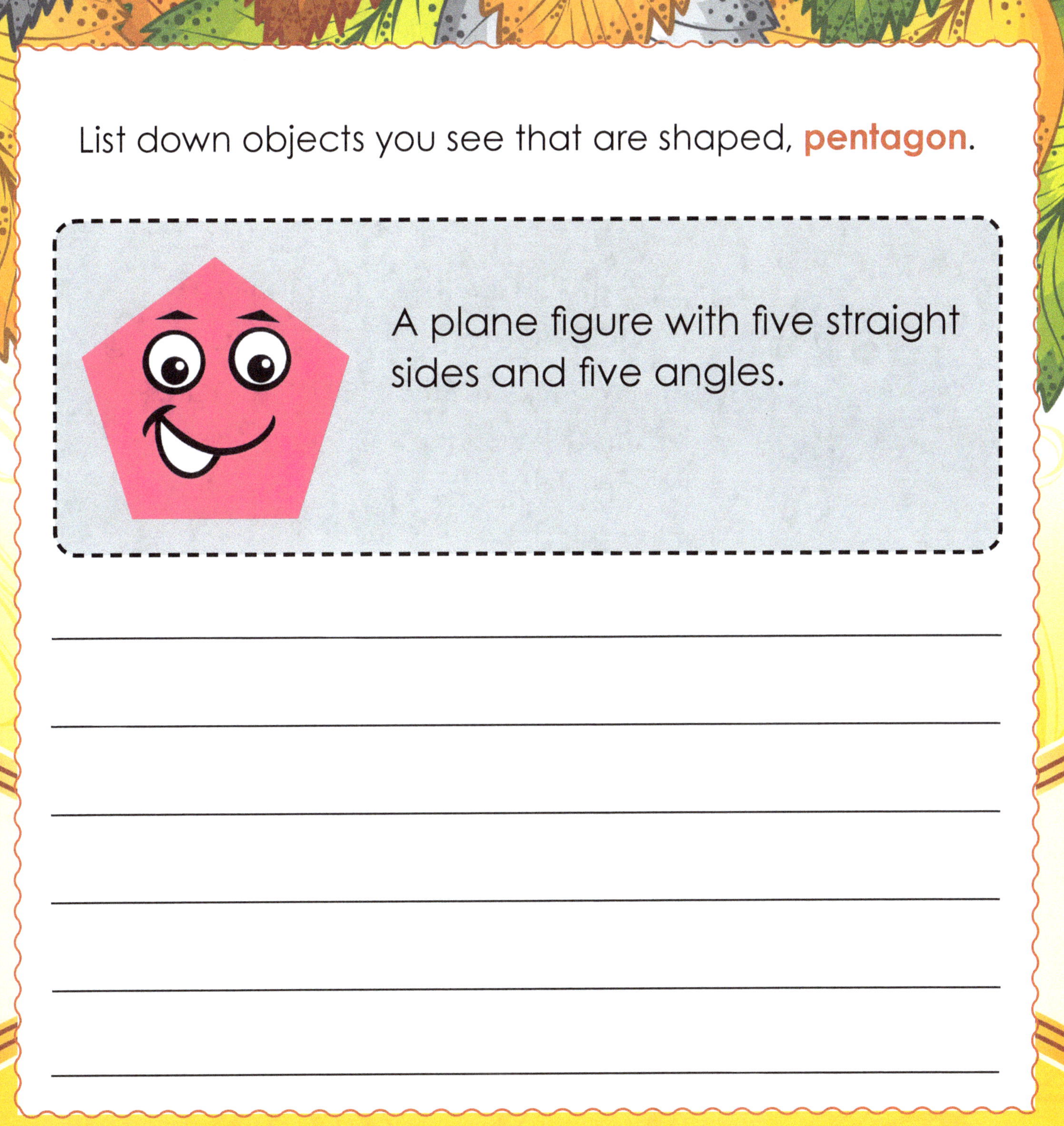

A plane figure with five straight sides and five angles.

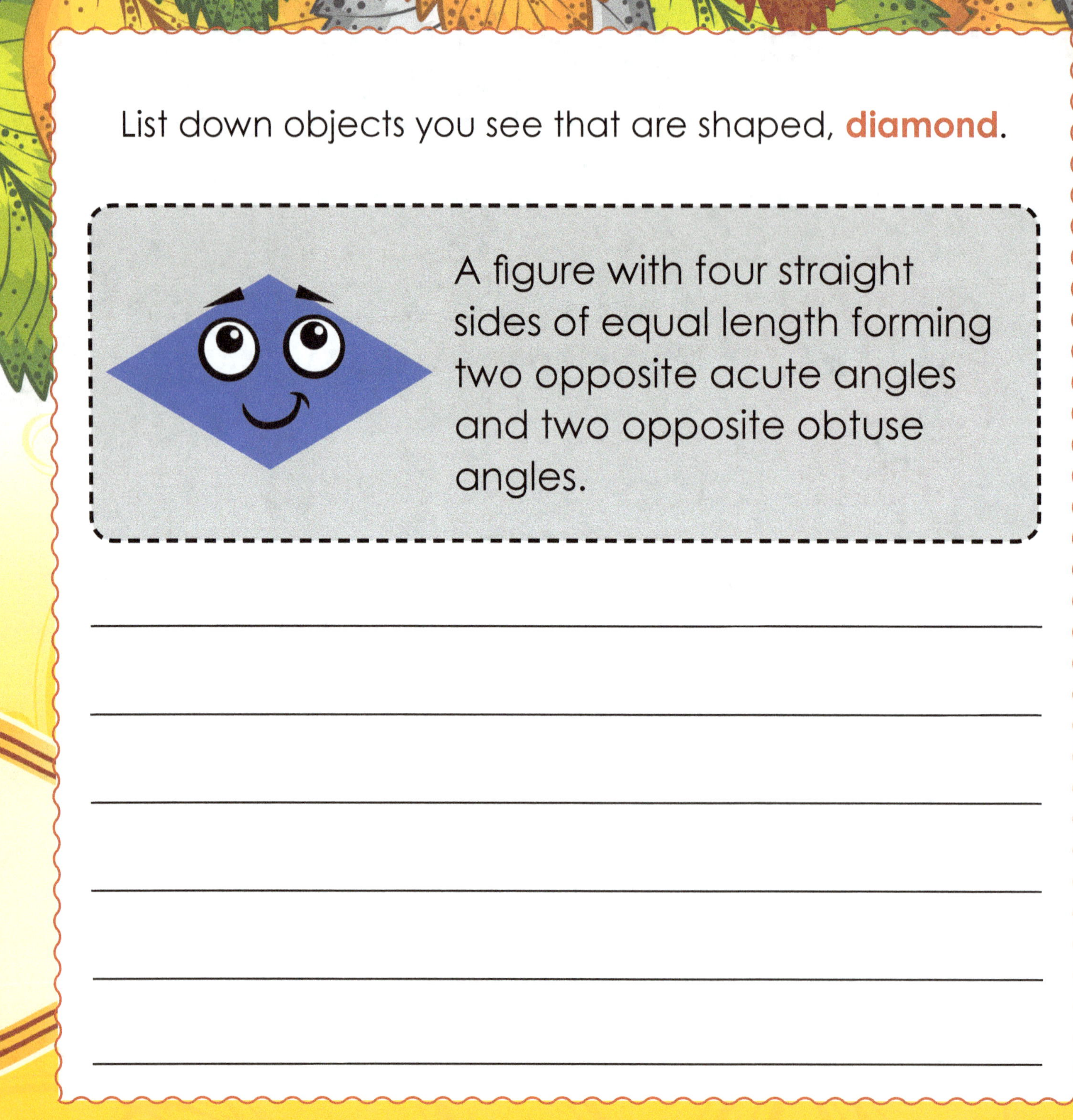

List down objects you see that are shaped, **diamond**.

A figure with four straight sides of equal length forming two opposite acute angles and two opposite obtuse angles.

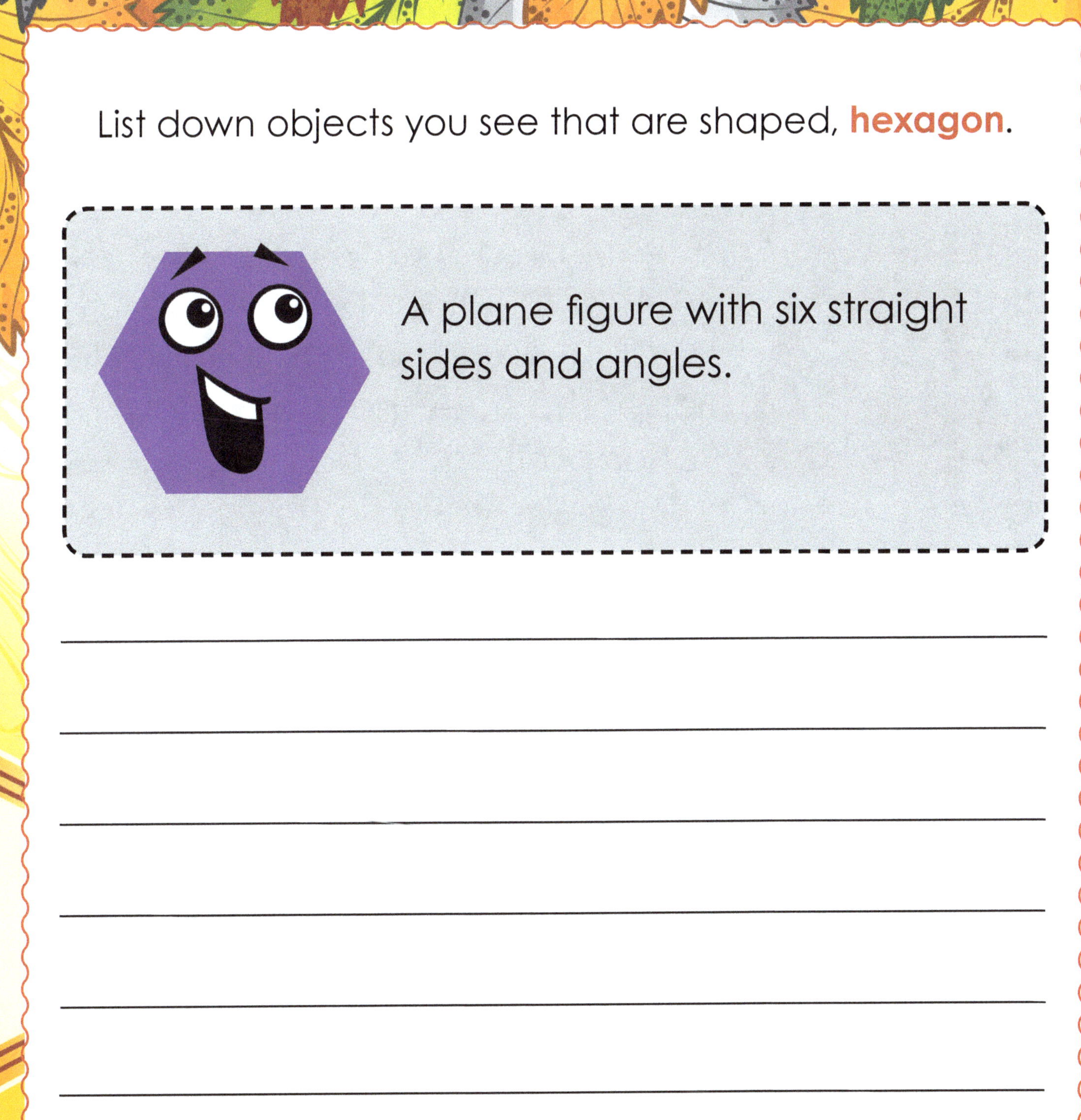

List down objects you see that are shaped, **hexagon**.

A plane figure with six straight sides and angles.

List down objects you see that are shaped, **trapezium**.

A 4-sided flat shape with straight sides that has a pair of opposite sides that has a pair of opposite sides parallel.

List down objects you see that are shaped, **star**.

A five-pointed polygons; a combination of 5 triangles and 1 pentagon.

____

____

____

____

____

____

List down objects you see that are shaped, **triangle**.

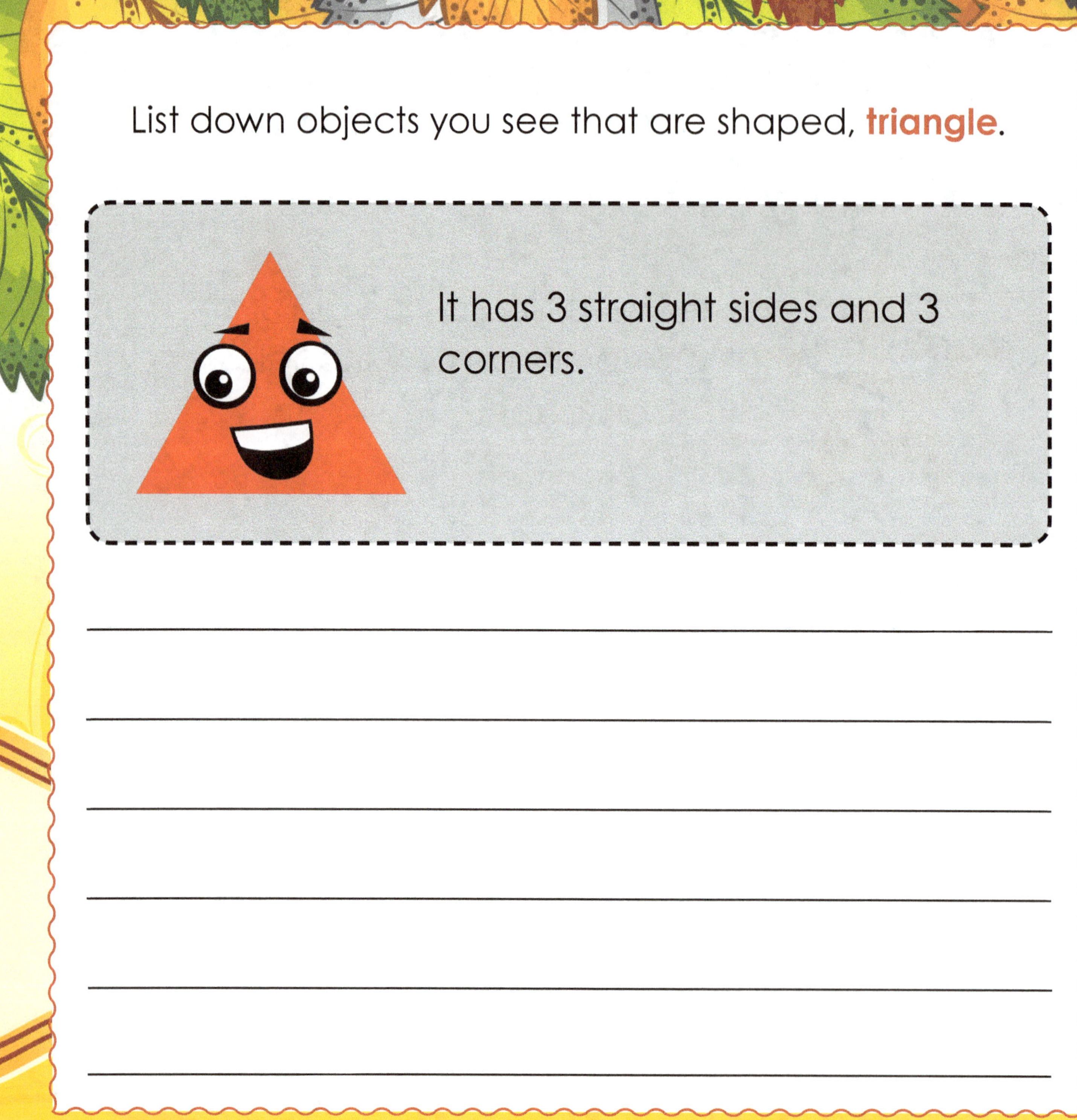

It has 3 straight sides and 3 corners.

List down objects you see that are shaped, cuboid.

A solid that has six rectangular faces at right angles to each other.

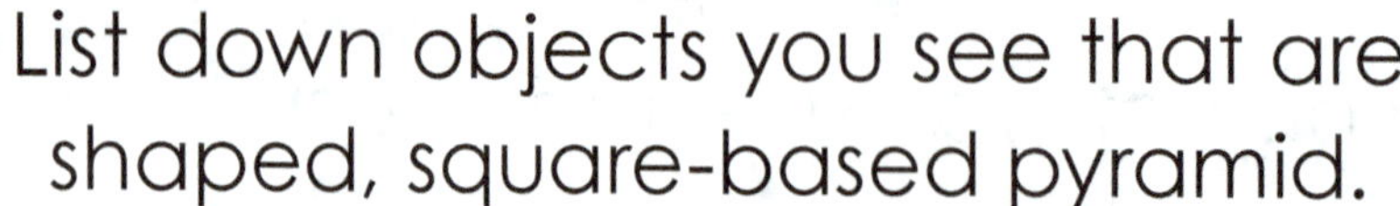

List down objects you see that are shaped, square-based pyramid.

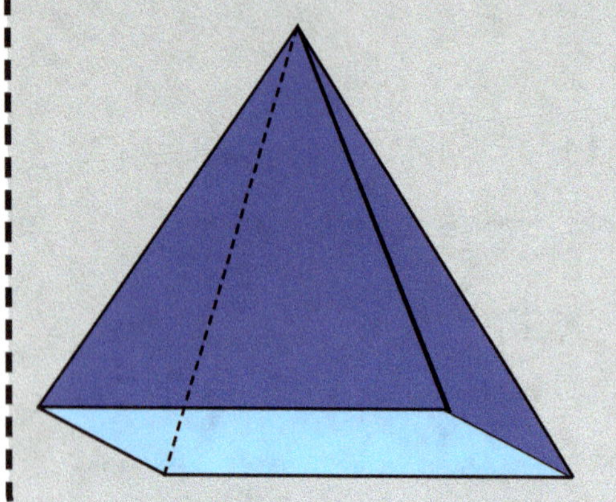

Is a pyramid having a square as base, it has 4 triangles on each side with same base width.

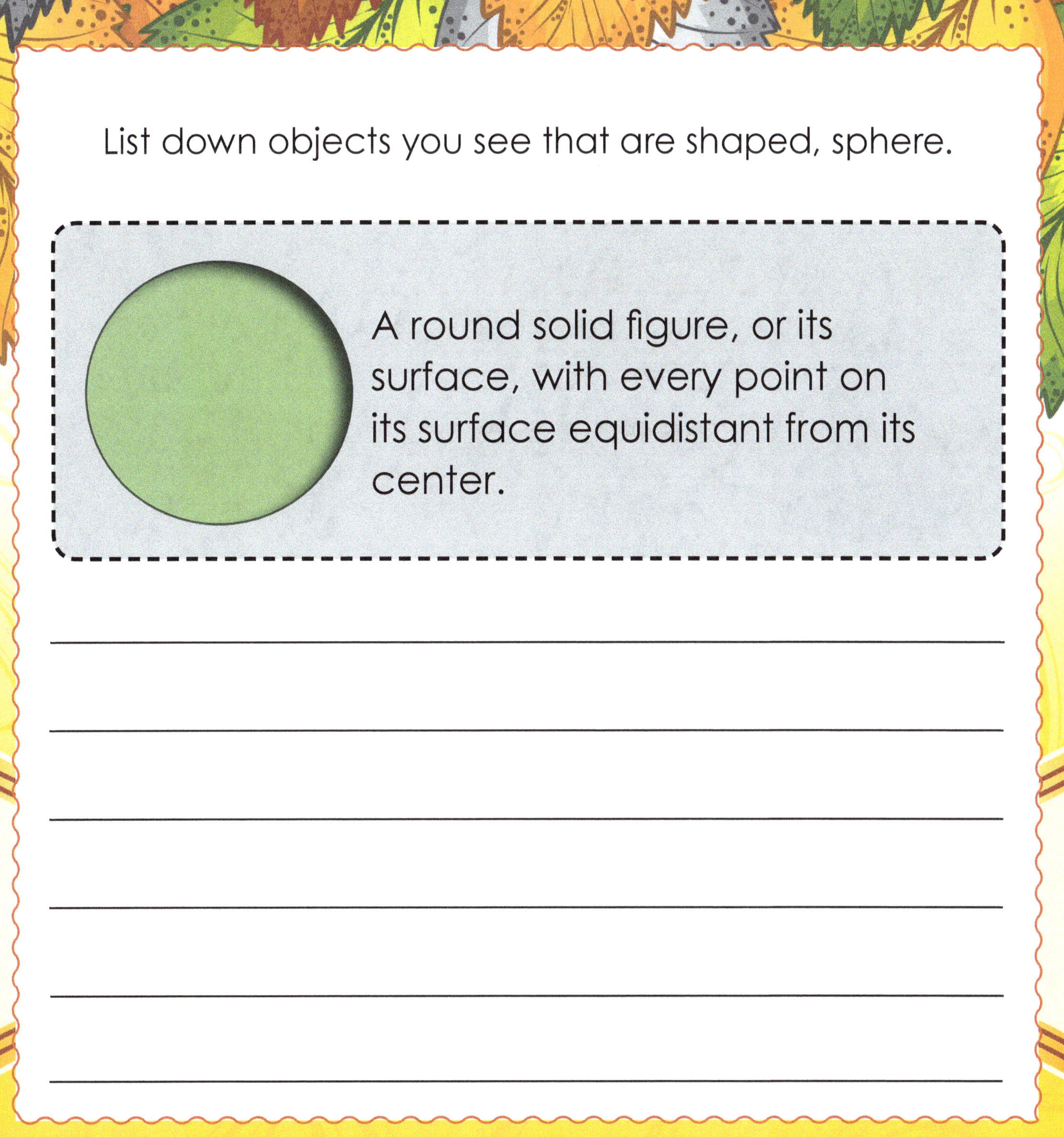

List down objects you see that are shaped, sphere.

A round solid figure, or its surface, with every point on its surface equidistant from its center.

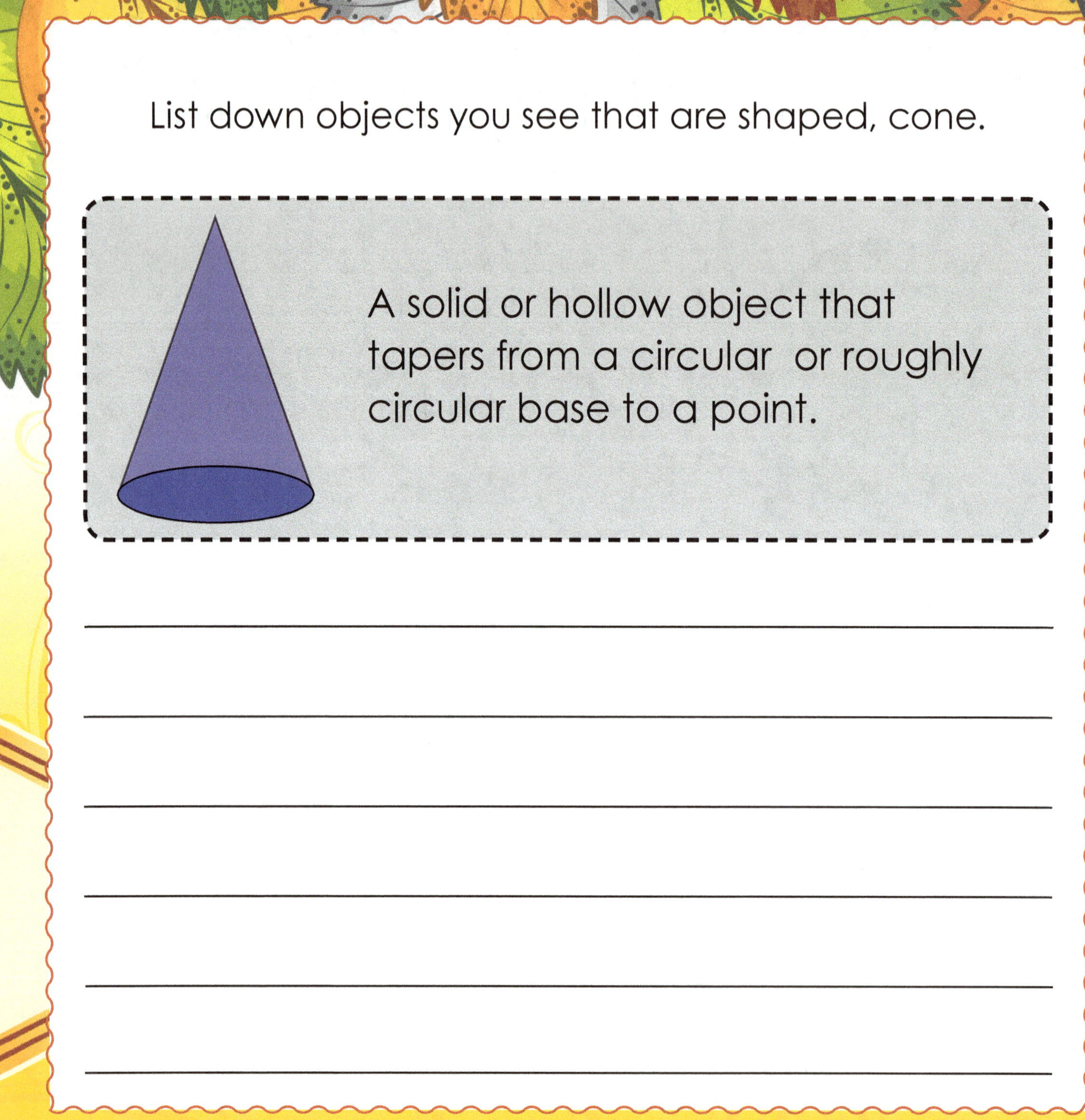

List down objects you see that are shaped, cone.

A solid or hollow object that tapers from a circular or roughly circular base to a point.

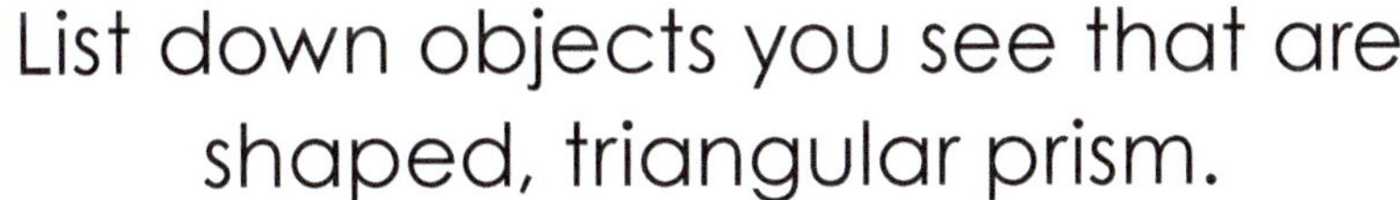

List down objects you see that are shaped, triangular prism.

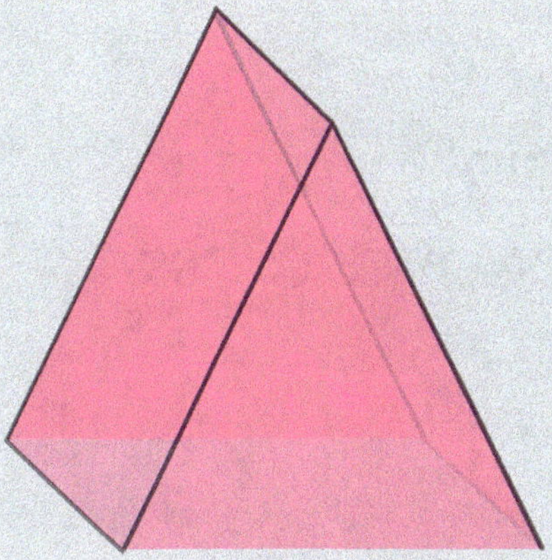

A prism made of 2 triangles and 3 rectangles.

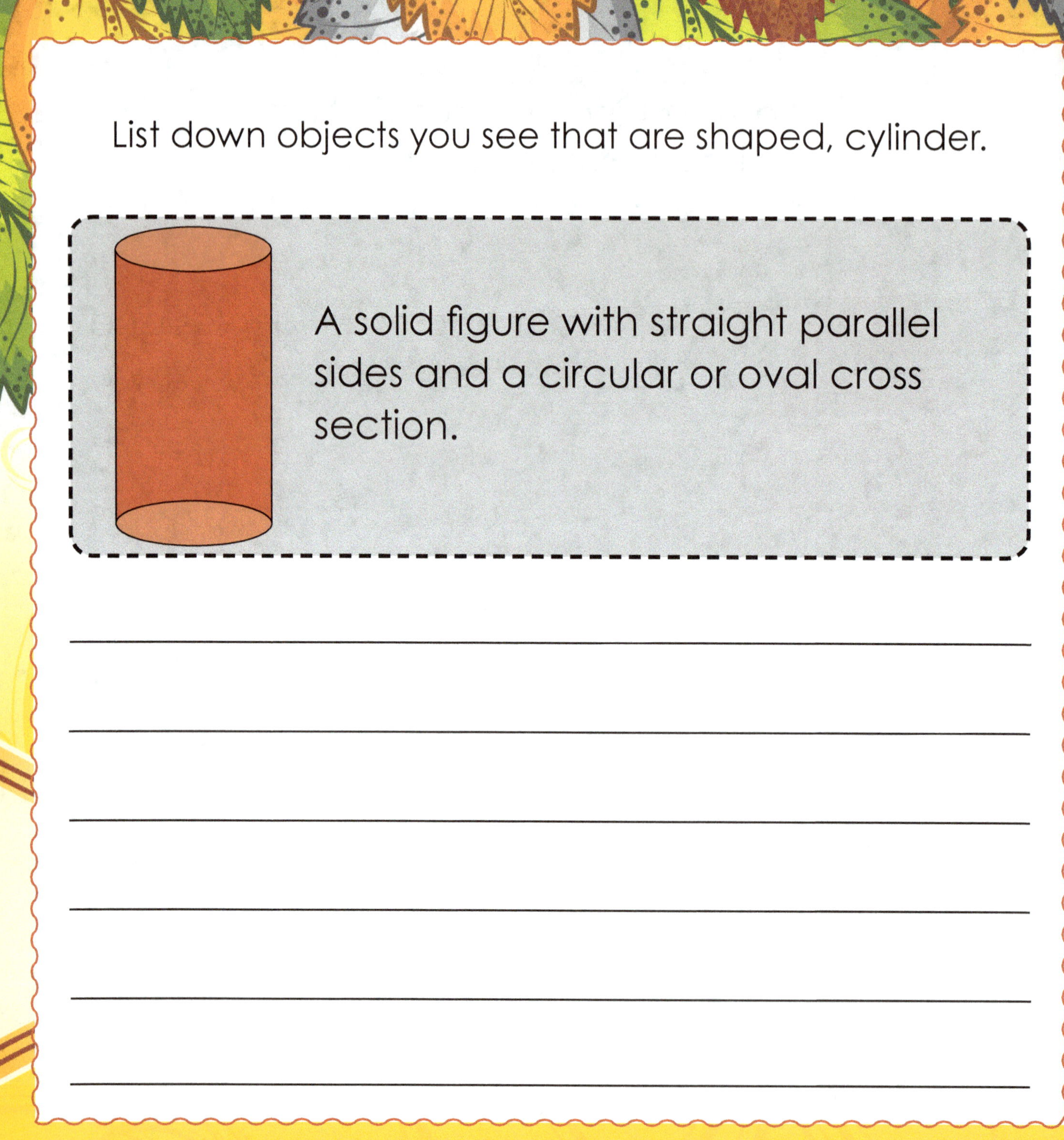

List down objects you see that are shaped, cylinder.

A solid figure with straight parallel sides and a circular or oval cross section.

List down objects you see that are shaped, cube.

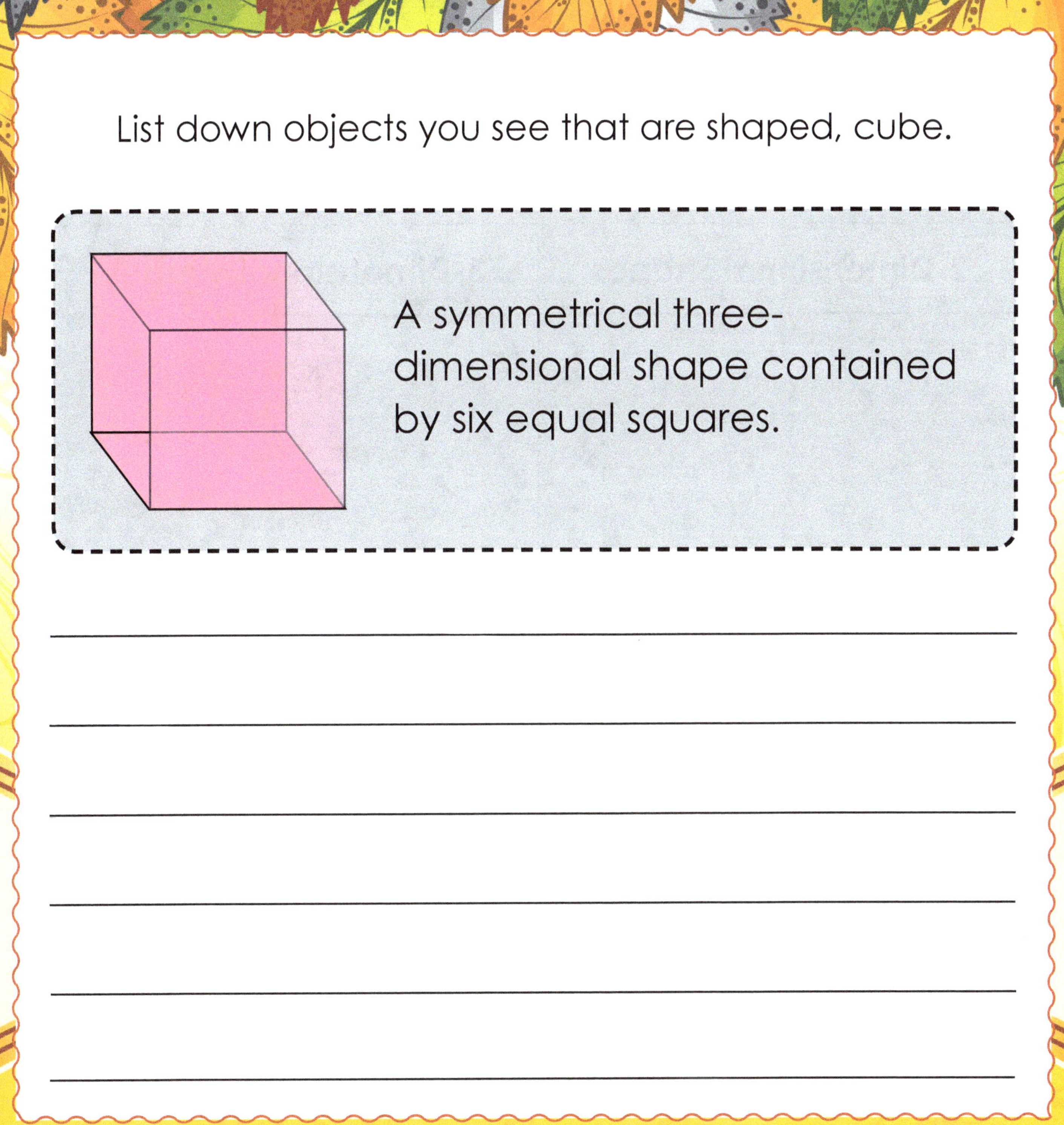

List down the 2-Dimensional and 3-Dimensional Shapes.

2-Dimensional Shapes	3-Dimensional Shapes

Angles

Identify what type of angle.

Acute Angle

An angle that is **less than 90°**.

Right Angle

An angle that **exactly 90°**.

Obtuse Angle

An angle that is **more than 90°** but **less than 180°**.

Straight Angle

An angle that is **exactly 180°**.

Reflex Angle

An angle that is **more than 180°**.

1. 113° ______________________________

2. 49° ______________________________

3. 65° ______________________________

4. 148° ______________________________

5. 223° ______________________________

6. 90° ____________________

7. 180° ____________________

8. 256° ____________________

9. 45° ____________________

10. 104° ____________________

11. 300° ____________________

12. 62° ____________________

13. 28° ____________________

14. 123° ____________________

15. 61° ____________________

Draw the angle.

1. 154°

2. 24°

3. 243°

Polygons

Draw the polygon.

1. Pentagon

2. Dodecagon

3. Hendecagon

4. Hexagon

5. Decagon

6. Heptagon

7. Octagon

8. Nonagon

www.ingramcontent.com/pod-product-compliance
Lightning Source LLC
LaVergne TN
LVHW060515170826
845677LV00026B/1759
* 9 7 9 8 8 6 9 4 5 4 8 8 1 *